ECHOES
OF THE
SOUL

NAMRITA JOUHAL LALLY

Paperback: 978-1-961438-18-7
eBook: 978-1-961438-19-4
Library of Congress Control Number: 2023909944

This book is a work of nonfiction.

Ordering Information:

Prime Seven Media
518 Landmann St.
Tomah City, WI 54660

Printed in the United States of America

"TO MY MOTHER, WHO TAUGHT ME TO SEE THE BEAUTY IN LIFE'S JOURNEY AND INSPIRED ME TO WRITE THESE WORDS FROM THE ECHOES OF MY SOUL."

As I embark on the introspective journey of reminiscing about my life, I am filled with a profound sense of humility. The tapestry of experiences that have woven themselves into the fabric of my being has shaped me in ways beyond measure. It is with great pleasure and vulnerability that I present to you this collection of poems, "Echoes of the Soul." Through these verses, I seek to encapsulate the myriad of emotions—joy, pain, love, and loss—that have reverberated through the chambers of my heart and soul.

This book is an homage, a heartfelt tribute to my beloved mother, whose unwavering love and steadfast support have been the guiding light illuminating my path. Her indomitable spirit and grace continue to ignite my spirit, providing solace and inspiration every day. I remain forever indebted for the gift of her life, a beacon of love and strength that has forever imprinted itself upon my soul.

To my dear sons, my eternal wellsprings of joy and the very essence of my existence, I offer these poems as tokens of wisdom and affection. As you traverse the labyrinthine corridors of life, may these verses serve as poignant reminders to cherish the beauty inherent in every fleeting moment. Through both triumphs and tribulations, may you find solace and inspiration in these echoes of my soul, allowing them to resonate harmoniously with your own, and guiding you towards a life illuminated by hope, compassion, and unwavering love.

Dear reader, I extend an earnest invitation for you to accompany me on this profound journey—a journey into the depths of our souls, where emotions ebb and flow like the tides of the ocean. Together, let us immerse ourselves in the timeless beauty and the ephemeral nature of life's precious instants. Let these words serve as a gentle reminder, a melodic whisper urging you to embrace each day as a precious gift, to dance with the symphony of existence, and to paint the world with hues of love, kindness, and boundless empathy.

With an abundance of love and unwavering gratitude that resonates deep within my being,

NamRita Jouhal

"RIDING THE WAVES OF EMOTIONS"

The waves crash over me,
In an endless ebb and flow,
I ride them like a surfer,
With nowhere else to go.

The thrill of the crest,
As I rise to the top,
The fear of the trough,
As I'm pulled to the drop.

Emotions like waves,
Come and go as they please,
I hold on tight and ride them out,
Until the turmoil ease.

Sometimes the water's calm,
And the waves gently roll,
Other times, a tempest rage on,
And I am powerless, all hope gone.

But I keep on riding,
Through the storms and the calm,
For the waves of emotions,
Are what makes life a psalm.

"THE EMOTION'S CREST"

Feelings are like waves upon the shore,
They ebb and flow forevermore.
Sometimes they're gentle, soft, and low,
Other times they rage and grow.

Love and joy, hope and peace,
These emotions bring us release.
Sadness, anger, fear and pain,
We try to avoid but can't restrain.

Feelings are what make us human,
They're the colours in life's broad spectrum.
Without them, life would be dull,
A never-ending, monochrome lull.

So let them come, and let them go,
Experience them high and low.
For in the end, it's what we feel,
That makes our existence real.

A BREATH OF SPRING

The air is crisp, the sky is blue,
As winter fades and spring breaks through.
The trees awaken from their sleep,
Their branches stretching, no longer steep.

The sun is warmer, the breeze is light,
As nature stirs from its quiet night.
The world comes to life once more,
As flowers bloom and birds explore.

A symphony of sound and hue,
As nature sings its song anew.
The grass grows greener, the earth awakes,
As winter's hold slowly breaks.

A breath of spring, a sign of hope,
As new beginnings help us cope.
With life's challenges, its ups and downs,
We find renewal in spring's sweet sounds.

So let us embrace this season of change,
And all the wonders it can arrange.
For life is but a fleeting thing,
And spring reminds us to spread our wings.

THE DANCE OF THE FIREFLIES

In the stillness of the night,
As darkness envelopes sight,
The fireflies come out to play,
In a magical, mesmerizing way.

With wings that glow like stars above,
They dance and flicker, showing love.
Their movements soft and luminescent,
A sight to see, so effervescent.

In unison, they twirl and sway,
A symphony of light at play.
A dance so graceful, free and wild,
Like a child's laughter, sweet and mild.

With each new move, they light the way,
Guiding us through the dark of day.
A reminder that in every gloom,
There's still a chance for life to bloom.

So let us cherish this enchanting sight,
The dance of fireflies in the night.
For in their light, we find our way,
Towards a brighter, happier day.

THE MAGIC OF BOOKS

Books are magic, I do believe,
For in their pages, we can conceive,
A world beyond what we can see,
A place of wonder, where we're free.

With every word, a new adventure,
A journey beyond our own departure.
Characters come alive in our mind,
Their stories weaving, one of a kind.

From mysteries to fantasies,
Romances to tragedies,
Books hold a power, so profound,
To take us to new worlds, unbound.

The pages turn, the story unfolds,
A universe of tales untold.
We lose ourselves within each page,
And find within, a solace, a sage.

Books are magic, in every way,
A place where we can laugh and play,
A haven from life's routine,
A realm where our souls convene.

So let us embrace this wonderland,
The magic of books at our command.
For within their pages, we can find,
A world of dreams, a peace of mind.

MELANCHOLY

The weight of sadness, heavy and deep,
A sombre veil that one can't keep.
Melancholy, a cloak of despair,
A state of being, hard to bear.

A sea of sorrow, a tide of tears,
A feeling that's been around for years.
A world of pain, an endless grief,
A heart that struggles to find relief.

The colours of life, once bright and bold,
Now seem to fade, like stories old.
The laughter that used to fill the air,
Now echoes faintly, lost in despair.

Melancholy, a state of mind,
That seems to leave no joy to find.
A weight that's heavy, hard to lift,
A struggle that seems to have no gift.

But even in the midst of all this gloom,
A ray of light can still find room.
A hope that flickers, a spark of grace,
That helps us move from this dark place.

So let us not be consumed by this weight,
But let us rise, before it's too late.
For even in the midst of sorrow,
We can find a way to live tomorrow.

THE PAIN OF SOLITUDE

The silence echoes, the stillness so loud,
As the pain of being alone enshrouds.
The world outside seems far away,
As the heart aches, day by day.

The emptiness inside is hard to bear,
A loneliness that seems unfair.
The longing for a companion near,
A desire that's hard to disappear.

The memories of laughter and cheer,
Now seem like a dream, so dear.
The echoes of love, once so strong,
Now seem like a distant song.

The pain of solitude is hard to break,
A weight that seems hard to shake.
But even in the midst of all this pain,
There's still a chance for love to reign.

For love can come in many forms,
A friend, a pet, or a partner warm.
A hand to hold, a shoulder to lean,
A companion to share life's dream.

So let us not be consumed by the pain,
But seek the light, before it's too late.
For even in the depths of loneliness,
There's still a chance for love and happiness.

BELIEVE IN YOURSELF

Believe in yourself, with all your might,
For in your heart, there's a shining light.
A strength that's deep, a power within,
That helps you rise, and let your journey begin.

The world outside may try to tear you down,
But don't let their words make you frown.
For you are strong, you have the will,
To overcome any obstacle, and climb any hill.

Believe in your dreams, let them soar,
For they hold the key to something more.
A world of possibilities, a life so true,
If you just believe, it will come to you.

The road may be long, the path may be tough,
But with every step, you'll become more than enough.
A force to reckon with, a shining star,
If you just believe, you'll go far.

So let your heart guide you, trust your soul,
For you are destined for a beautiful goal.
Believe in yourself, with all your heart,
And you'll find that you've had the power from the start.

STRONGER THAN YOU KNOW

When the road ahead seems rough,
And the path you take feels tough,
Remember that you're stronger than you know,
With the power to overcome and let your light glow.

The trials you face may seem too great,
But remember that you hold the key to your fate.
You have a strength that's deep within,
A power that will help you rise and win.

The world outside may try to bring you down,
But you have the strength to wear the crown.
A champion of your own destiny,
With the power to set yourself free.

You are stronger than you know,
With the ability to make your dreams grow.
So hold your head up high and believe,
For the strength you need, you already conceive.

With every challenge, you grow more,
And become a stronger version of what you were before.
So let the struggles help you rise and soar,
And let your strength be your guiding force forevermore.

For you are stronger than you know,
With the power to conquer and let your light show.
Believe in yourself, trust your might,
And you'll find that everything will be all right.

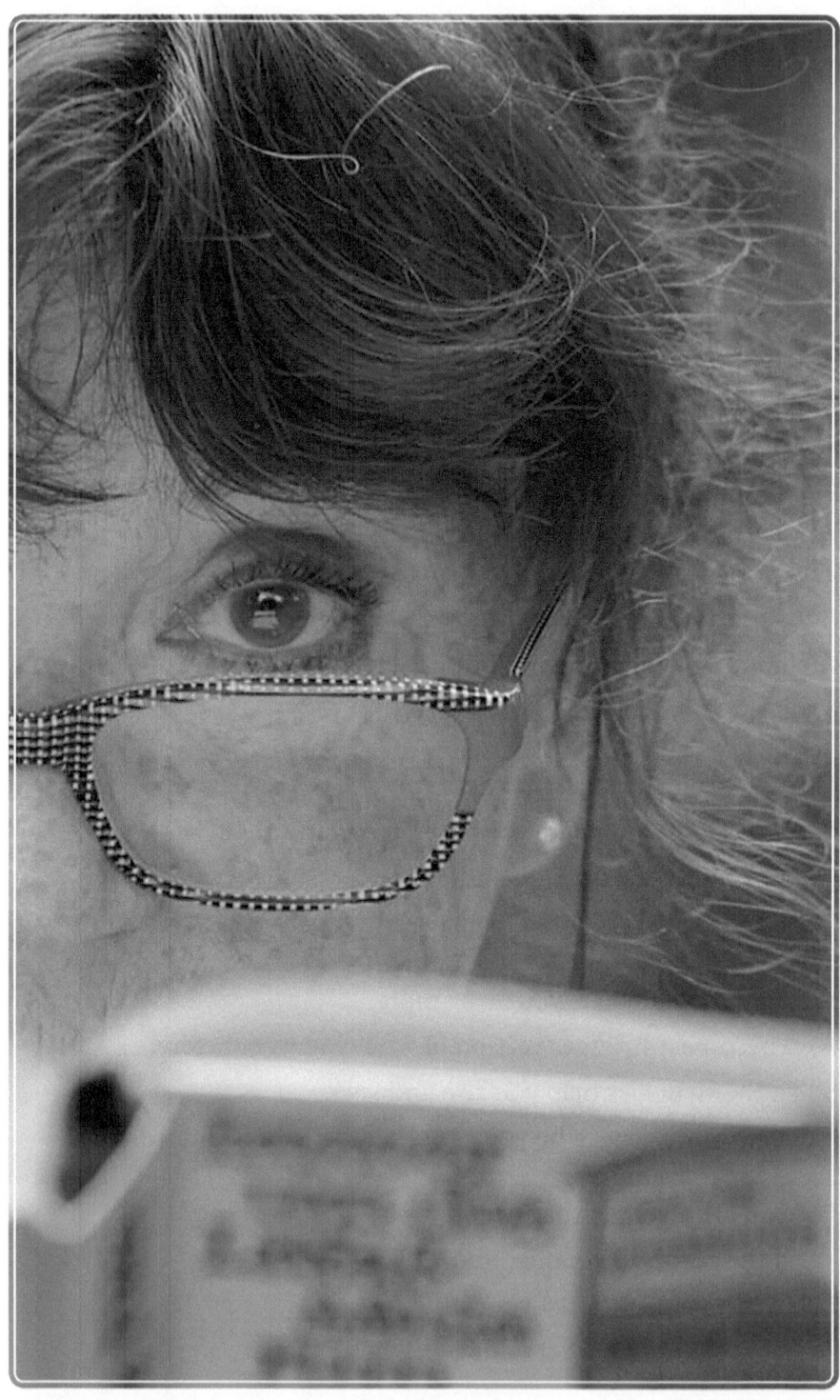

DO NOT JUDGE

Do not judge a book by its cover,
For there's so much more to discover.
The pages within hold the key,
To a story that's waiting to be set free.

The world outside may seem so quick,
To judge and label, and make it stick.
But there's a beauty in every soul,
That shines so bright, it makes us whole.

The labels we use, the boxes we create,
Only serve to separate and alienate.
For in the end, we are all the same,
With different stories, but the same flame.

So let us not be quick to judge,
But instead, let's extend a loving nudge.
Let's open our hearts, and listen with care,
For the stories we hear, have the power to repair.

For every soul we meet, there's something new,
A lesson to learn, a different view.
So let us not judge, but embrace,
For in the end, it's love that we should chase.

Do not judge a book by its cover,
For there's so much more to discover.
Let's open our hearts, and let love flow,
And watch as a beautiful world begins to grow.

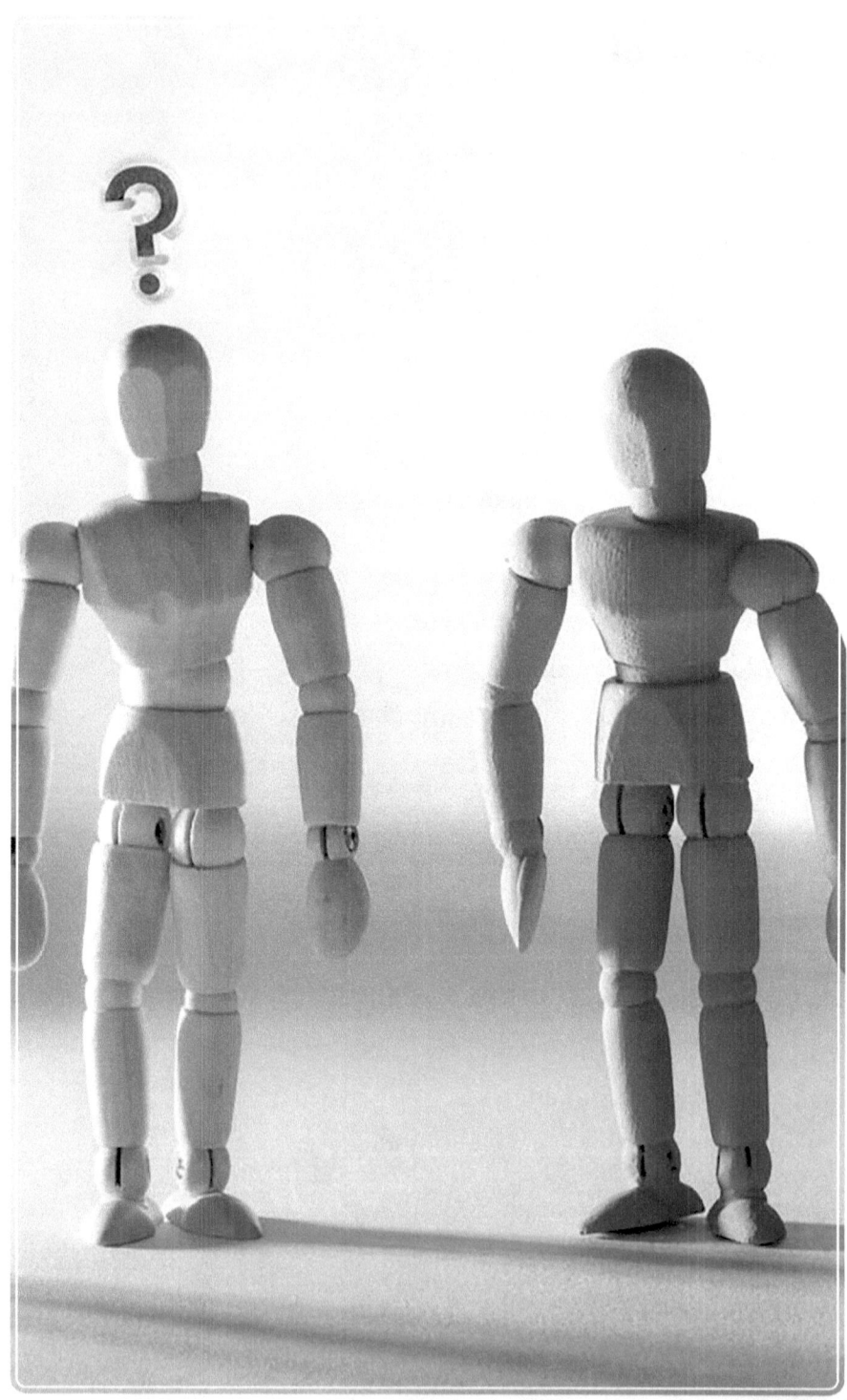

QUICK TO JUDGE

We're quick to judge, it's true,
We see the surface and make assumptions anew.
We look at others with a critical eye,
And often fail to see the reasons why.
We judge based on race, gender, or creed,
And forget that every person has a unique need.
We label and stereotype without a second thought,
And in doing so, our own ignorance is wrought.
But why are we so quick to judge and condemn?
Is it out of fear or a need to feel like we're on top of them?
Perhaps it's because we've been conditioned to think a certain way,
Or because we lack the empathy to understand what others say.

you know as well as I,
Judging others can cause pain and make us sigh.
It's important to remember that everyone has their own story,
And that our judgments can hinder their path to glory.

So, let us strive to be mindful and kind.
To put ourselves in others' shoes with an open mind.
Let's seek to understand and learn,
So that our judgments don't cause others to burn.

For in the end, we're all human, and we're all flawed,
But we can choose to love, to empathize, and to applaud.
And together, let's make a world of different hues,
Where everyone is celebrated, and no one's a ruse.

CHOOSE TO LOVE

In a world full of hate and strife,
It's easy to get caught up in the fight.
We see the differences that divide,
And forget the common ground on which we can abide.

But amidst the chaos and confusion,
There's a choice that's ours to make: to choose love as our solution.
To look beyond the labels and the hate,
And see the human being, the soul behind the face.

For love has the power to heal and unite,
To bridge the gaps and bring the light.
It sees the beauty in every being,
And sees the potential in everything.

To choose love is not always easy,
For it requires vulnerability and humility.
It means setting aside our own pride,
And seeing the world through a different set of eyes.

But when we choose to love, we open the door,
To a world of possibility and so much more.
We see the potential for peace and harmony,
And we become part of a movement towards a brighter destiny.

So let us choose love, every day,
And let it guide us along the way.
For in the end, it's love that will win,
And bring us closer to the world we've been dreaming in.

DREAM FOR REAL

Close your eyes and dream with me,
Of all the things that you want to see.
The world is yours, it's all in your mind,
Let your imagination be unconfined.

Dream of mountains, and oceans wide,
Of journeys that take you far and wide.
Dream of love, and a life fulfilled,
Of all the adventures that will make your heart thrilled.

But dreams alone won't make it real,
It takes hard work and a steely will.
It takes courage to chase what you desire,
And perseverance to keep going when things get dire.

So let your dreams fuel your passion,
And let your heart guide your action.
Take the first step, and then the next,
And before you know it, you'll be far from the text.

For dreams are not just a figment of the mind,
They can be real if you're willing to grind.
So go on, my friend, chase your dream,
And watch as it becomes your reality, supreme.

For when you dare to dream for real,
The world opens up to you, with zeal.
You become the master of your fate,
And life becomes an adventure that's great.

WANDERING MIND

My mind wanders like a bird in flight,
Soaring over hills and mountains, taking in the sight.
It drifts away like a leaf on the wind,
And before I know it, I'm lost in its spin.

It takes me to places far and wide,
To the depths of the ocean, and the other side.
It shows me worlds beyond my own,
And takes me to places I've never known.

But sometimes it leads me astray,
And I lose my focus and forget the way.
I get lost in the endless sea of thought,
And forget the world that I'm meant to be caught.

It's a strange feeling, to be in two worlds at once,
One in my mind, and one in the present, at once.
But it's a reminder that the mind is a powerful tool,
And if I use it well, I can achieve more than I thought I could.

So I take a deep breath and focus my gaze,
And bring my wandering mind back to the present days.
For it's in the here and now that life truly unfolds,
And it's in the present that true beauty and joy is told.

But I'm grateful for my wandering mind,
For it shows me the world in a different kind.
It helps me see beyond the surface of things,
And takes me on adventures on eagle wings.

MIND OF AN OVERTHINKER

My mind is a labyrinth, a maze of thoughts,
A never-ending cycle, a battle that can't be fought.
It's a place where logic and reason collide,
And where doubt and uncertainty always reside.

I overanalyse every move I make,
Every decision I take, every step I take.
I question everything, from the mundane to the grand,
And I can't help but worry, it's out of my command.

I replay conversations over and over,
Analysing every word, every phrase, like a lover.
I second-guess every move I make,
Wondering if I did enough, if there's more at stake.

It's a constant battle between my mind and heart,
One pushing me forward, the other tearing me apart.
I'm trapped in this web of endless thought,
And it's a struggle to break free, to find what I sought.

But in the midst of all the chaos and noise,
There's a glimmer of hope, a ray of poise.
For in the end, it's the mind that creates,
And it's the power of thought that shapes our fates.

So I'll take a deep breath and calm my mind,
And let my thoughts flow, unrestrained and kind.
For it's in the space of quiet and calm,
That my mind can rest, and I can find my charm.

BETRAYED

Why does it seem like every time,
I try to trust, I'm left behind.
Why does it seem like every bond I make,
Is just another chance for someone to break?

I've been let down, left to fall,
Betrayed by those I thought would stand tall.
It's a bitter pill to swallow, a tough lesson to learn,
That not everyone is deserving of the trust I yearn.

But still I try, and still I hope,
That someday I'll find a way to cope.
That someday I'll find someone who's true,
Someone who won't betray me through and through.

It's not easy to trust when you've been hurt,
It's not easy to open up when you've been burnt.
But I'll keep on trying, keep on pushing through,
For I know that someday, my heart will find someone new.

So to those who've betrayed me, I say this:
You may have hurt me, but you won't define me, miss.
For I am stronger than the pain you've caused,
And I'll rise above, with dignity and poise, applause.

Betrayal may sting, and trust may be tough,
But I won't let it break me, for that's not enough.
For in the end, it's love that triumphs over all,
And I'll keep on searching, till I find my call.

TRUTHFUL LIES

Sometimes the truth is hard to tell,
And so we weave a web, a spell.
We spin our words, craft our tales,
And hope that our lies don't leave trails.

But what if the truth is a bitter pill,
A pill that we just can't fulfil?
What if the truth is too much to bear,
And so we resort to a lie to spare?

A truthful lie, a lie that's true,
A lie that's meant to help us through.
A lie that's wrapped in a kernel of fact,
A lie that's meant to protect and impact.

It's a dangerous game, this truth and lie,
A balance that's tough to satisfy.
For every lie, we risk the truth's decay,
And every truth, we risk the lie's dismay.

But still we choose to play this game,
For it's the only way to keep our shame.
We choose to deceive, to hide and mask,
For fear of what the truth will unmask.

So we tell our truthful lies, our lies that ring true,
And hope that somehow, they'll see us through.
For in the end, it's the truth that sets us free,
But sometimes a lie is what we need to see.

BETRAYED TRUST

Was it the betrayal or the trust that hurt the most,
When I found out what I had lost?
Was it the lies or the truth that broke my heart,
When I realized we were worlds apart?

I thought I could trust you with my soul,
But you broke that trust, left a gaping hole.
You played me for a fool, with your deceit and lies,
Left me with a shattered heart, and tears in my eyes.

But was it the betrayal that hurt me so,
Or the trust that I gave, with nothing to show?
For in the end, it was my trust that you stole,
Leaving me with nothing, but a broken soul.

I thought I knew you, thought you were true,
But in the end, I was just a pawn to you.
You used me for your gain, and threw me aside,
Leaving me with nothing but a heartache to abide.

So was it the betrayal or the trust that hurt the most,
When I found out what I had lost?
In the end, it was the trust that I gave away,
That left me with nothing, but a price to pay.

JUST A MIRAGE

You came into my life like a mirage,
A vision of beauty that I couldn't dodge.
You promised me love, you promised me light,
And for a moment, everything felt just right.

But as time went by, I began to see,
That you were just a mirage, nothing more than a fantasy.
Your love was empty, your promises a lie,
And I was left alone, wondering why.

You lured me in with your seductive gaze,
And I fell for you, like a moth to a flame.
But now I see that it was all a game,
A cruel trick, with no one to blame.

You were just a mirage, a trick of the mind,
A fantasy that I was foolish enough to find.
But now I know the truth, I see it clear,
That you were never real, just a mirage I held dear.

So I'll move on, and leave you behind,
For I know now that you were just a trick of the mind.
I'll find someone real, someone true,
And I'll be happy, without the need for you.

I STILL TALK TO YOU

Even though you're gone, I still talk to you,
As if you were here, like we used to do.
I tell you about my day, my hopes and fears,
And sometimes I imagine that I can hear your cheers.

I know you're not here, not in the flesh,
But sometimes it feels like you never left.
Your memory lingers, like a gentle breeze,
And sometimes I feel your presence, like a comforting ease.

I know I can't see you, or hear your voice,
But still, I talk to you, as if I have a choice.
For in my heart, you still remain,
A part of me, that will never wane.

So I'll keep talking to you, as if you're still here,
Sharing my joys, and sometimes my tears.
For even though you're gone, your spirit lives on,
And in my heart, you'll never be truly gone.

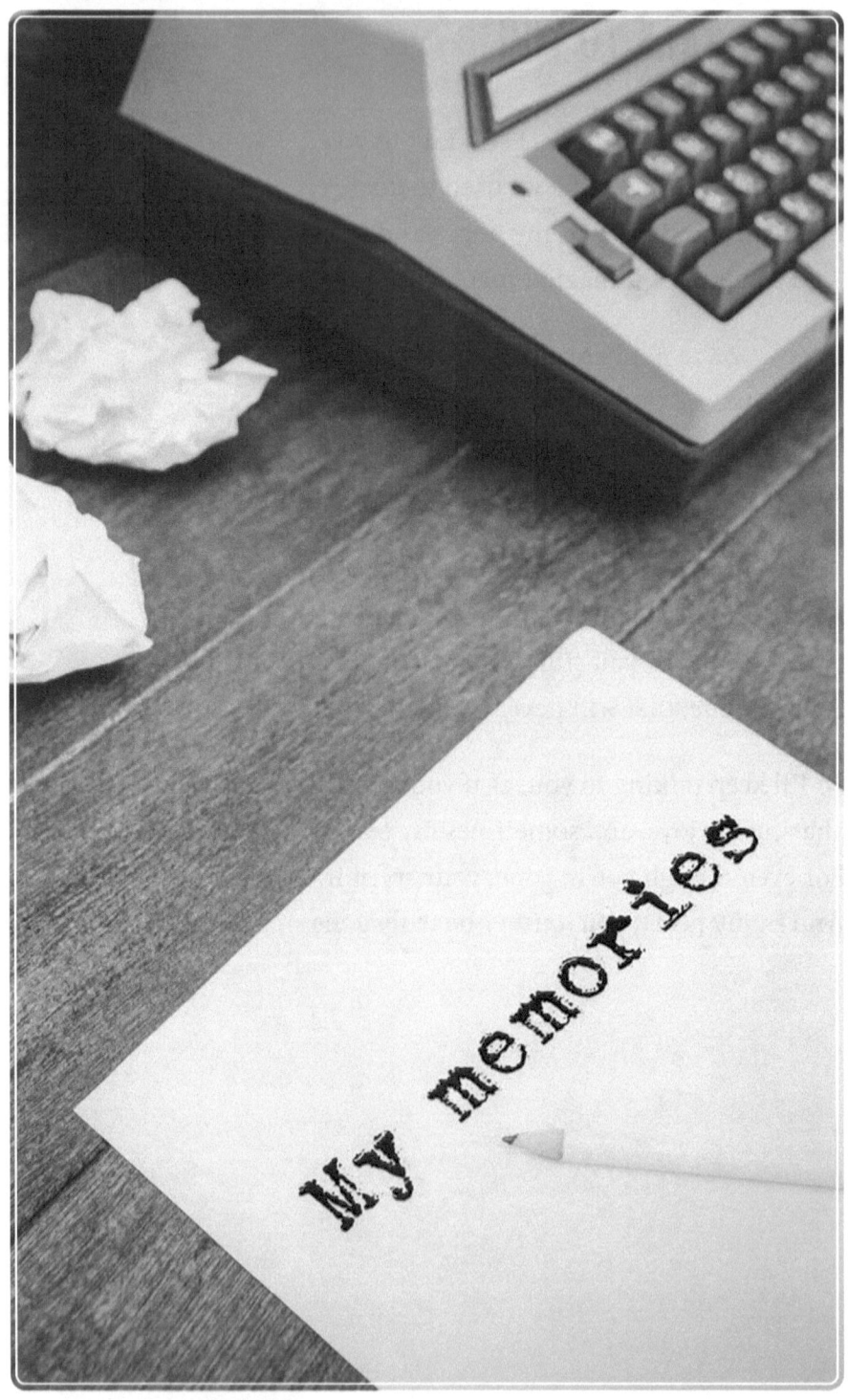

LINGERING MEMORIES

Memories of you, they linger still,
In the corners of my mind, where they always will.
The scent of your perfume, the sound of your voice,
Remind me of a time, when I had a choice.

A choice to love, to hold you close,
To cherish every moment, like a precious rose.
But now you're gone, and all that remains,
Are memories of you, like a sweet refrain.

Sometimes I close my eyes, and see your smile,
And for a moment, it's like we're back in style.
But then reality sets in, and I'm alone once more,
With nothing but memories, to cherish and adore.

Memories of you, they linger still,
Like a bittersweet pill, that I can't help but swallow.
But even though you're gone, and time marches on,
Your memory will remain, like a sweet song to follow.

ENERGY OF LOVE

Love is a powerful energy,
It flows like a river, it's always in motion.
It can lift you up, or bring you down,
It can make you feel like you're floating on a cloud.

Love is an energy that can heal,
It can mend broken hearts, and make you feel whole.
It can fill you up, and make you feel alive,
It can give you strength, and help you survive.

Love is an energy that can ignite,
It can light a fire, and make your heart take flight.
It can spark a passion, and light up your soul,
It can make you feel complete, and make you whole.

Love is an energy that can transform,
It can change you, in ways you never thought possible.
It can make you see the world in a new light,
And give you the courage, to take flight.

So cherish the energy of love,
Let it flow through you, like a gentle dove.
Let it lift you up, and bring you joy,
And let it be your guide, your constant ally.

YOU GIVE ME COMPANY EVEN THOUGH YOU ARE GONE

You may be gone, but you're not forgotten,
Your memory lingers on, like a warm embrace.
You give me company, even though you're gone,
And I find comfort in the memories we've made.

I close my eyes, and I can see your face,
The sound of your laughter, your tender embrace.
The memories we've shared, they'll never fade,
For in my heart, they will always be saved.

You give me company, even though you're gone,
And I feel your presence, like a guiding light.
I know that you're with me, in spirit and soul,
And that gives me the strength, to carry on.

Though you may be gone, you're never far away,
For the memories we've made, will always stay.
And so I find comfort, in the love we've known,
And in the fact that you give me company, even though you're gone.

LOSING A MOTHER

Losing you was like losing a part of me,
A piece of my heart, that I'll never retrieve.
You were my rock, my guiding light,
And now that you're gone, it feels like night.

The world seems a little dimmer, a little less bright,
Without your presence to light up my life.
I miss your smile, your gentle touch,
The way you always knew just what I needed, and when.

But even though you're gone, your love lives on,
In every memory, every moment we shared.
Your legacy lives on, in the person I've become,
And I know that you're proud, wherever you are.

I may have lost you, but I'll never forget,
The love you gave me, the lessons you taught.
And so I'll keep your memory alive, in everything I do,
And know that you're watching over me, from up above.

BEREFT

I'm lost and alone, adrift in the world,
Since the day you left, and my heart was unfurled.
Bereft of your guidance, your love, and your care,
I'm struggling to cope, and it just doesn't seem fair.

Your memory lingers, like a warm embrace,
But it's hard to hold on to, in this cold and lonely space.
I miss your smile, your laughter, your touch,
The way you made everything seem not so much.

The world keeps moving, but I'm standing still,
Wishing for just one more moment, one more thrill.
But though you're gone, your love lives on,
In every memory, every thought, every dawn.

I'll always be bereft, without you here by my side,
But I'll keep your memory alive, with every step, every stride.
And though the pain of your loss will never quite subside,
I'll find comfort in knowing you're always there, watching over me
with pride.

GUIDING ME THROUGH LIFE

Guiding me through life, it is you mom,
Even though you're gone, I feel your calm.
Your wisdom and guidance, still guide my way,
And I find solace in the memories that will forever stay.

Though it's hard without you, I carry on,
With the strength and love that you have passed on.
I see you in the sunrise and the sunset's glow,
And feel your presence in every breeze that blows.

You taught me to be brave, to never give up,
To always see the best in people, and to never hold a grudge.
Your lessons and your love, will forever remain,
A guiding force in my life, through joy and through pain.

So thank you, dear mom, for all that you've done,
For shaping who I am, and for helping me become.
You'll always be with me, in spirit and in heart,
Guiding me through life, even though we're apart.

YOUR PRESENCE ALWAYS LINGERS

Whenever something goes right, I know it's you, mother,
Your presence always lingers, even though we're far apart from each other.
You taught me to be strong, to never give up the fight,
And to always have hope, even when the world seems dark as night.

I see you in the sun's warm rays, and in the twinkling stars at night,
And I feel your love in every moment, in every triumph and in every plight.
You guide me through life, even though you're gone,
And I carry your love with me, as I journey on.

Though it's hard to carry on without you by my side,
I find strength in the memories that we shared, and in the love that will never subside.
Your wisdom, your love, your courage, they all remain,
A guiding force in my life, even when things seem mundane.

So thank you, dear mother, for all that you have done,
For making me who I am today, for helping me to become.
Your spirit lives on in my heart, and I'll always know it's true,
That whenever something goes right, it's because of you.

SIGNALS FROM THE UNIVERSE

The universe sends you signals, if only you would see,
Guiding you towards your destiny, setting your spirit free.
It whispers in the wind, and sings in the rain,
And you can hear its messages, if you just listen again.

It speaks in the language of the heart, and in the rhythms of the soul,
Guiding you towards your purpose, and making you feel whole.
It sends you signs and symbols, in the most unexpected ways,
And you can see them clearly, if you open your eyes to the rays.

The universe is always speaking, but are you willing to hear?
Are you ready to listen, and to face your fears?
It wants you to be happy, and to live a life that's true,
So it sends you signals, to guide you through.

So pay attention to the whispers, and heed the call of your heart,
The universe will guide you, and never let you fall apart.
Its messages will light your path, and keep your spirit bright,
And you'll know that you're never alone, as you journey through the
night.

THE SECRET WHISPERS OF THE WIND

The wind whispers the secret, in a language of its own,
A message from the universe, that's meant for you alone.
It carries with it a promise, and a sense of hope and light,
Guiding you towards your purpose, and to take flight.

It tells of hidden mysteries, and of wonders yet unseen,
Of a life full of potential, and of dreams waiting to be gleaned.
It speaks of a path that's true, and of a destiny in store,
Of the endless possibilities, that lie just beyond your door.

The secret whispers of the wind, can be heard by those who listen,
By those who trust in the journey, and in the wisdom that glistens.
It brings a sense of peace, and a knowing deep within,
That you're exactly where you're meant to be, and that's where the
magic begins.

So let the wind embrace you, and let it take you on a ride,
For the secret it whispers, is meant for you to abide.
It holds the key to your heart, and to a life that's meant to be,
And the winds of change will carry you, to a place of destiny.

THE PROTECTION OF NIGHT

When the world grows dark, and the stars appear,
The protection of night begins to draw near.
It wraps around you like a soft, warm embrace,
And shields you from the troubles of the day's race.

The moon shines bright, and the sky grows still,
As the worries of the world begin to chill.
The darkness brings a peace, that's hard to find,
As the noise of the day, fades out of mind.

In the quiet of the night, the soul can rest,
And find a sense of peace, amidst the day's unrest.
It's a time for reflection, and for finding grace,
As the protection of night, keeps the worries at bay.

So let the night envelop you, and let it be,
A time to find your center, and to simply be.
For in the silence of the night, the heart can hear,
The whispers of the soul, that are always near.

And when the morning comes, and the light breaks through,
You'll emerge with a new sense of strength and renew.
For the protection of night, will have given you,
The power to face the day, and to see it through.

BREAKING FREE FROM THE COCOON OF LIES

Just when I thought I was trapped in the cocoon of lies,
The world around me grew dark, and I couldn't see the skies.
But then a spark within me ignited, and began to glow,
And the light it gave me, helped me find a way to grow.

I broke free from the webs of deceit, that held me down,
And I began to see the beauty, in the world all around.
I spread my wings and flew, towards the heavens above,
And I knew that I was finally, free to find my love.

The cocoon of lies, that had once held me tight,
Became a distant memory, in the shadows of the night.
And in its place, a new life began to bloom,
Filled with hope and wonder, that would never consume.

So when you find yourself, trapped in the cocoon of lies,
Just remember that the light within you, never really dies.
It waits for you to find it, and let it lead the way,
Towards a life of truth and love, that's brighter every day.

BLESSED BY THE SUNLIGHT

The dense shadows of society's jungle,
Threaten to consume us whole,
And we feel lost and helpless,
In a world that takes its toll.

But just when we think we're trapped,
In the darkness of the night,
The rays of sunlight bless us,
With their warmth and gentle light.

They shine upon our faces,
And we feel their loving embrace,
As they guide us through the jungle,
And help us find our place.

We push through the thickets and the thorns,
And we emerge into the clearing,
With a newfound sense of purpose,
And a hope that's worth the hearing.

For the sunlight blesses us,
And it gives us strength to go on,
Through the ups and downs of life,
Until our battles are won.

So when you feel lost in the jungle,
And the shadows are closing in,
Just remember the sunlight's blessing,
And the hope it brings within.

DARE TO DREAM

You can make it happen,
If you can dare to dream,
To believe in yourself,
And let your spirit gleam.

The world is full of possibilities,
If you're willing to take the chance,
To step outside your comfort zone,
And join the cosmic dance.

It takes courage to pursue your dreams,
And to face your doubts and fears,
But the reward is worth the effort,
And the happiness it brings is clear.

So let your imagination soar,
And let your heart be your guide,
For within your dreams lies the power,
To achieve what you've always desired.

Dare to dream, and take the leap,
Into the unknown and the new,
For with each step you take,
The universe aligns with you.

STRENGTH WITHIN

When I thought I can do it no more,
And my spirit felt so weak,
I looked within and found the strength,
That I had been seeking all week.

For deep within us lies a power,
That we often don't realize,
A strength that can carry us through,
Even when life is full of surprise.

It's the resilience that we possess,
The courage that we hold so dear,
And when we tap into its power,
We can conquer any fear.

So when the world feels too heavy,
And the burden's hard to bear,
Just remember the strength within you,
And how much you truly care.

For the power that you possess,
Is greater than you know,
And with each day that you rise up,
You let that strength glow and grow.

So hold onto that inner fire,
And let it light your way,
For when you trust in yourself,
You can conquer any day.

VOICES WITHIN

The voices or vices that I had to overcome,
Were the whispers that held me back,
The doubts and fears that clouded my mind,
And left my soul feeling so off-track.

But I knew that I was stronger,
Than the demons that lurked within,
And with each step I took forward,
I could silence them and let my light in.

It took courage to face my fears,
And to confront the lies I told,
But the more I challenged those voices,
The more I found my inner gold.

For within us all lies a strength,
That can conquer any foe,
And with each victory we claim,
We let that inner light glow and grow.

So when the voices or vices return,
And try to knock us down,
Just remember the power within you,
And let that inner light abound.

For you are stronger than you know,
And with each step you take,
You can overcome those inner demons,
And find the path to your own fate.

PROVING THEM WRONG

Just when they said I was good for nothing,
I felt my spirit start to break,
The weight of their words heavy on my heart,
I wondered how much more I could take.

But deep within me, there was a fire,
A passion that refused to die,
And with each insult and each put-down,
It burned even brighter, reaching for the sky.

For I knew that I was more than just words,
More than the judgments they cast my way,
And I refused to let their negativity,
Dictate the course of my every day.

So, I set out to prove them wrong,
To show them all what I could do,
And with each step I took forward,
I left their doubts and fears behind me too.

And though it wasn't always easy,
And I stumbled more than once or twice,
I kept on pushing, kept on striving,
Never giving up or losing sight.

And in the end, I proved them wrong,
For I became everything they said I couldn't be,
And in that triumph, I found my strength,
And set my spirit free.

TRAPPED

The bird with wings, they told her to fly,
But the world outside was fraught with danger,
And so she kept to her cage, dreaming of the sky,
Afraid to venture forth, to embrace her true nature.

They said it was for her own protection,
That she was safer inside where they could see,
But every day, her wings grew weaker,
Her spirit dimmed, her dreams set free.

For what good were wings, if they couldn't soar?
What use were dreams, if they couldn't be realized?
And so she cried out to the world beyond,
A plea for help, a desperate compromise.

And one day, her cage was opened,
And she stepped out into the sun,
Her wings aching but determined,
To fly, to live, to be one.

But it was too late, her wings too weak,
And as she lifted off the ground,
She felt herself falling, falling,
To the world below, with a tragic sound.

And as she lay there, broken and shattered,
She realized the true cost of her fear,
For in holding herself back, in staying trapped,
She'd lost everything that she held dear.

So let this be a lesson to all of us,
To spread our wings, to fly, to be bold,
For though the risks may be great,
The reward is worth more than gold.

CAGED IN THOUGHTS

She lived in the cage for so long,
That she thought it was her only home.
With every passing day and night,
The walls grew thicker and her spirit light.

Her heart ached for freedom,
Her soul yearned to soar.
But the cage held her captive,
And her dreams felt so far.

Then one day, the cage door opened wide,
And she felt the wind, the sun, and the sky.
But fear crept in, and she froze in place,
She couldn't bring herself to leave that space.

She had grown so used to the cage,
It had become her safe haven, her refuge.
Even though she longed to be free,
The familiar seemed easier to see.

So she stayed near the cage,
Still feeling its invisible hold.
But deep down, she knew it was time,
To take a step forward, to be bold.

With a deep breath, she spread her wings,
And soared higher than she ever knew she could.
The freedom she felt was worth the risk,
And she realized that she had misunderstood.

For the reward of breaking free,
Was worth more than gold or any treasure.
She was finally living, truly alive,
And that was the ultimate measure.

KINDNESS

A single act of kindness,
Can light up a soul,
It can ease the pain,
And make a broken heart whole.

A gentle touch, a loving word,
Can go a long way,
It can lift someone up,
And brighten their darkest day.

Kindness grows the spirit,
It nurtures and it heals,
It can bring hope and joy,
To those who suffer and feel.

In a world so full of chaos,
And darkness all around,
A little bit of kindness,
Is like a ray of sunshine found.

So let us spread kindness,
Wherever we may go,
For it can make a difference,
More than we will ever know.

For kindness is contagious,
It spreads like wildfire,
And when we give it freely,
We light up the world with love and desire.

"EPHEMERAL BEAUTY"

In the morning mist,
I catch a glimpse of you,
A fleeting vision,
Of ethereal beauty true.

Your radiance shines,
In the soft sunlight,
A delicate bloom,
A wondrous sight.

Your petals unfold,
In a dance so fine,
A moment in time,
An ephemeral design.

For like all beauty,
Your time is brief,
A fragile creation,
A transient belief.

But though you fade,
And fall to the ground,
Your memory lingers,
In my heart profound.

For you are a reminder,
Of the beauty we share,
A gift to be cherished,
A moment rare.

And though you are gone,
Your essence remains,
In the world around us,
In nature's refrain.

For you are the beauty,
That we hold so dear,
A reminder of life,
Of what we hold near.

SACRED KNOWLEDGE

In ancient texts and whispered lore,
Lies knowledge sacred, hidden and more,
A wisdom passed from age to age,
On dusty pages and ancient sage.

The secrets of the universe revealed,
In cryptic texts and symbols sealed,
Mysteries that few can comprehend,
A journey of the soul, without an end.

The whispers of the sages old,
A sacred knowledge, pure as gold,
Of love and light, of truth and grace,
A path that leads to a higher place.

Through trial and pain, through dark and light,
A sacred journey, an inner fight,
To find the truth, to seek the way,
To hear the voice that leads to day.

In sacred knowledge, we find the light,
A path that leads to pure insight,
A journey of the heart, the mind, the soul,
A quest to find the ultimate goal.

HEART'S JOURNEY

Journey of my heart, it's been long and winding,
Full of twists and turns, at times so blinding.
The path has been rocky, the hills so steep,
But my heart keeps moving, it never does sleep.

I've travelled through valleys, so deep and so low,
Felt the weight of despair, with nowhere to go.
But then came the sunrise, the dawn of a new day,
And my heart found its footing, it started to sway.

I've seen the beauty of love, felt its gentle embrace,
And the pain of heartbreak, the tears on my face.
But my heart remains strong, it keeps on beating,
For it knows that each step is a lesson worth heeding.

Through it all, I've learned to trust in my heart,
To listen to its whispers, to never be apart.
For the journey of my heart is one of grace and love,
And it will keep on going, soaring high above.

ECHOES OF PAST

Lost in the echoes of yesterday,
Memories that haunt and never fade away,
Moments of joy, now distant and grey,
A soul that longs to break free and stray.

In the stillness of the night,
The heart aches with all its might,
For the days that were bright,
And the dreams that took flight.

The past is a weight hard to bear,
A burden that one cannot help but share,
The moments that slip away without a care,
Leaving behind a soul lost in despair.

But hope still flickers, a tiny flame,
A glimmer of light in a life of pain,
A chance to rise up from the ashes again,
And heal the wounds, to ease the strain.

So let go of the echoes that bind,
Leave behind the shadows of the mind,
Embrace the present, let your heart unwind,
And a new dawn, a new life you will find.

"RISING ABOVE ADVERSITY"

When life throws challenges upon challenges,
And the road ahead seems endless,
The heart may falter, the mind may reel,
But the will to survive, it cannot steal.

The storm may rage, the winds may howl,
But the spirit will not bow or cower,
For within us lies a strength so true,
A resilience that sees us through.

The obstacles may seem insurmountable,
The path may be dark and formidable,
But with each step, the light grows brighter,
And the will to keep going, it burns even stronger.

The fight is hard, the journey long,
But we press on, we stay strong,
For the dream that drives us, it keeps us alive,
And the hope that sustains us, it never dies.

And in the end, we may be battered and worn,
But we stand victorious, our spirits reborn,
For we have faced the worst and come out alive,
And nothing can break the will to survive.

So let the challenges come, one by one,
For we are warriors, our battles won,
And with each victory, our souls shine bright,
A testament to the strength of the human fight.

THE ALCHEMY OF SOLITUDE

In the quiet of my solitude,
I find a peace that's hard to include,
A calmness that flows through my being,
And a sense of serenity that's freeing.

The magic of being alone but not lonely,
Is in the alchemy that's slowly,
Transforming the emptiness of my heart,
Into a richness that's a work of art.

For in the stillness of my mind,
I find a sanctuary that's one of a kind,
A place where I can leave behind,
The worries that burdened my soul and mind.

And in this sacred space,
I find the beauty of grace,
The inner wisdom that I can embrace,
And the love that fills every empty space.

For it's in the solitude of my heart,
That I find the magic of a new start,
And the strength to face life's every part,
With a courage that never falls apart.

So here I stand, alone but not lonely,
In the magic of my solitude, wholly,
With a heart that's free and holy,
And a soul that's one with the divine solely.

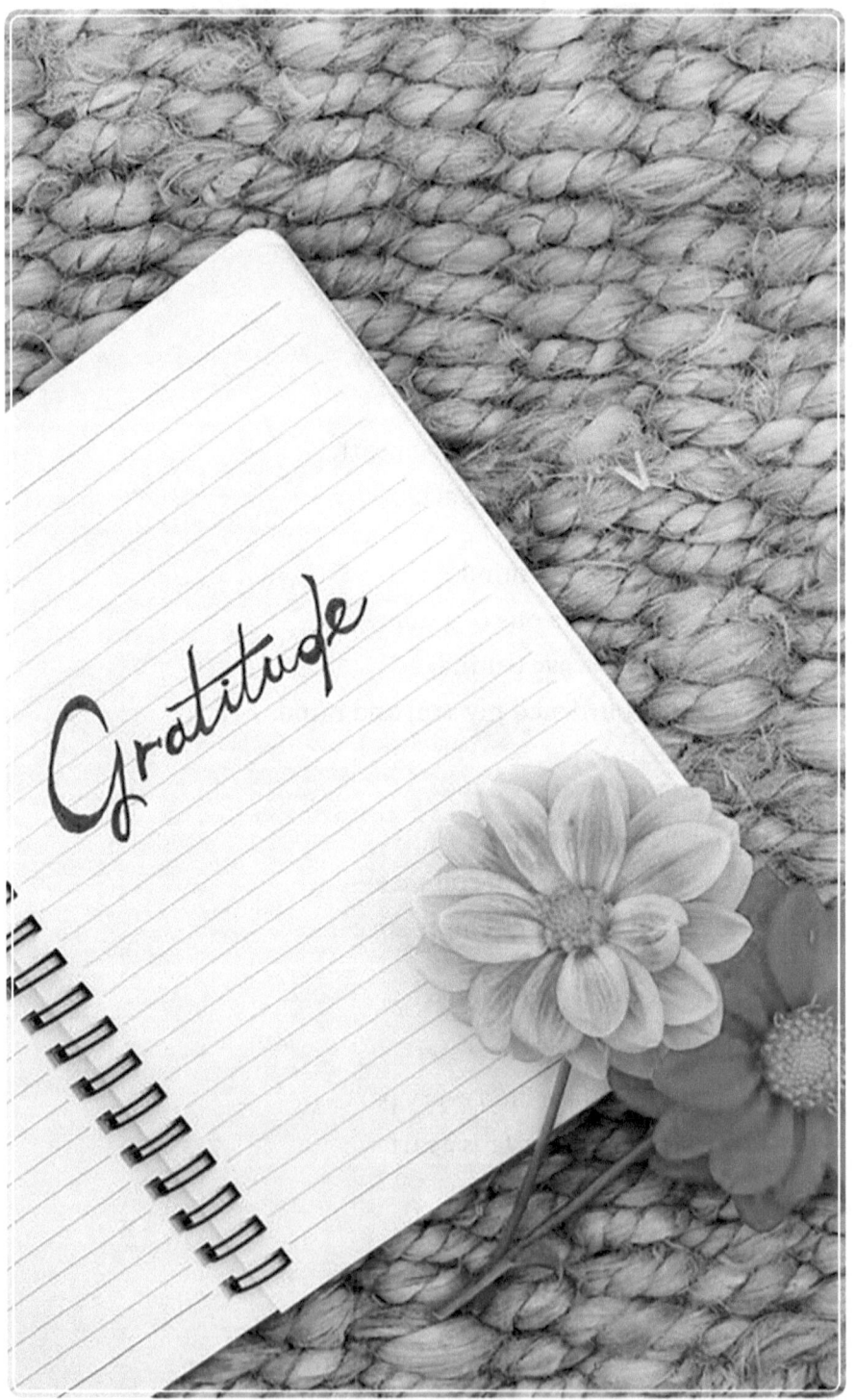

"GRATITUDE TO GRACE"

Grace, the gift that we are blessed to receive,
A force that guides us through life's journey,
A light that shines when we grieve,
A comfort in moments of uncertainty.

With grace, we learn to forgive and forget,
To embrace the beauty of each new day,
To cherish the moments that we have left,
And to find the courage to face what comes our way.

For every step we take on this earth,
We are granted grace in countless ways,
Through the love of family and friends,
Through the kindness of strangers each day.

So let us give thanks for the grace we receive,
And let it fill our hearts with joy and peace,
For it is a precious gift, beyond belief,
A miracle that we should never cease to cherish and appreciate.

For in the end, it is the grace that we are given,
That helps us find our way, no matter where we may roam,
And it is the gratitude in our hearts that keeps us driven,
To continue on, to live, to love, and to call this earth our home.

"SUNFLOWER'S EMBRACE: A SYMBOL OF STRENGTH AND SUPPORT"

In the fields of gold, they stand tall and bright,
A sight to behold, a true delight,
Their faces turned towards the sun,
A symbol of hope, a life that's begun.

As the day fades and the sun goes down,
They turn to each other, their heads bow,
Sharing their energy, their strength and might,
Through the darkest of nights, they shine bright.

Like sunflowers, we too can face,
The challenges of life, with gratitude and grace,
We can turn to each other, find support and light,
And together, we'll make everything right.

Let us learn from the sunflowers, the way they grow,
Bringing warmth and love, letting our light show,
Let us face each other, and share our energy,
And live a life, filled with joy and synergy.

For in this world, we need each other,
To grow, to thrive, to love one another,
So let us face each other, with hearts full of love,
And let the world know, we are guided from above.

TRUST THE TEST OF LIFE

Life may throw me challenges,
And put me through great tests,
But I'll keep my faith unshaken,
And trust that I'll do my best.

The path ahead may be unknown,
And the journey may seem tough,
But I'll keep my heart wide open,
And my spirit strong enough.

I'll face the storms with courage,
And the darkness with a light,
I'll embrace the twists and turns,
And trust that things will be alright.

For every hurdle that comes my way,
I'll take it as a chance to grow,
And with each step that I take,
I'll trust the journey and the flow.

For life is a test of strength and will,
And I know I'll make it through,
If I keep my heart and mind aligned,
And trust the journey that is due.

So I'll face each day with a smile,
And let my faith be my guide,
For I trust the test of life,
And know that I'll thrive and shine.

THE PARADOX OF LOVE

The ones that were meant to love me,
Hurt me and left me in agony,
Their words and actions, a constant injury,
Leaving me in a state of misery.

But the ones I did not know,
Showed me love and kindness that did glow,
Their hearts open wide like a rainbow,
Bringing me warmth and a love that did grow.

Life is a paradox of love,
It comes from unexpected places like a dove,
Sometimes it hurts, but it also gives,
Teaching us to forgive, to love, to live.

So I'll let go of the pain and the hurt,
And embrace the love that did avert,
I'll cherish the ones that gave love with no reserve,
And the ones that hurt me, I'll let them serve.

For in the end, love is what matters most,
It's what we give, and what we boast,
So let love be the one that guides us close,
And let the paradox of love be our host.

LESSONS FROM BETRAYAL

The ones I loved and trusted so,
My heart and soul I did bestow,
But they repaid with cruel blows,
And left my spirit filled with woe.

I gave them all I had to give,
My time, my love, my will to live,
But in the end they chose to sieve,
And through the holes my heart did sieve.

The world now sees me as a foe,
A villain in their twisted show,
But little do they truly know,
The hurt and pain I undergo.

I set my boundaries, stood my ground,
But they could not bear to hear the sound,
Of their own flaws so tightly bound,
And to me they dealt a final round.

Betrayed, I stand with head held high,
For I know in my heart, I did not lie,
I gave my all, and though they deny,
I will heal and rise above the lie.

EMBRACING IMPERFECTION

With every scar and every flaw,
I learn to love myself more,
For though I'm not perfect, that's for sure,
I am worthy of love, of that I'm sure.

I used to hide behind a mask,
Pretend to be someone else, an impossible task,
But now I know, to be myself is all I need to ask,
And from there, a life of joy and love can bask.

I've made mistakes, oh so many,
But with each one, I learn plenty,
And with each lesson, I grow strong and steady,
A better version of myself, I am becoming steadily.

So I embrace my imperfections, every single one,
For they make me unique, like the rising sun,
And with each day, I strive to be someone,
Who spreads love and light, until my time is done.

THE BUTTERFLY'S BLISS

The butterfly flutters by,
Unaware of its beauty in the sky,
Blinded by its own disguise,
It fails to see its worth and prize.

Its wings of vibrant hue,
A sight that stuns and wows anew,
Yet the butterfly remains subdued,
Lost in thoughts, it cannot pursue.

The world around it stops to stare,
In awe of the butterfly's wings so rare,
But the butterfly does not seem to care,
For its own beauty, it is unaware.

Oh, butterfly, open your eyes,
See the world through a new guise,
Let go of your own disguise,
And embrace your beauty with open skies.

For in your wings lies a story untold,
A tale of beauty that must be told,
So spread your wings and take hold,
Of the beauty that you truly behold.

A WARRIOR'S JOURNEY

Through the darkness, I push on,
A warrior's heart, though weary and worn,
Struggling with pain and mental strain,
Yet, I carry on, with strength I've gained.

The weight of the world, heavy on my back,
But for my loved ones, I will not crack,
With each step, I face my fears,
And wipe away my endless tears.

The battle within, a constant fight,
Days when I yearn to take flight,
But I cling to hope and hold on tight,
For a brighter day, beyond the night.

My scars, a testament to my will,
Each wound, a reminder of my uphill,
But I rise up, with a warrior's skill,
And march on, with a heart that still.

Through all my trials and endless pain,
My journey has become a steadfast chain,
Linked by strength and resilience, not in vain,
For I am a warrior, and I shall sustain.

"THE RADIANCE OF INNER JOY"

Happiness within, a precious gem,
A joy that shines from deep within,
A light that guides, a soothing balm,
That eases the pain and heals the skin.

It's not a treasure that can be bought,
Or found in a place that can be sought,
But within oneself, it must be wrought,
A journey within, a lesson taught.

It's the beauty of a kind heart,
The warmth of a gentle start,
The courage to make a brand new start,
And the strength to never fall apart.

Happiness within, a priceless gift,
That fills the soul and helps it lift,
Above the struggles and the rifts,
Towards a future bright and swift.

So cherish it well and nurture it strong,
Let it guide you through the right and wrong,
And when life's journey is finally done,
Happiness within, will forever shine on.

THE CROSSROADS OF LIFE

Life is a journey, so they say,
But which path should we take each day?
Do we go with the flow and let it be,
Or look for directions that will set us free?

At times the road ahead seems clear,
And we walk with purpose and without fear,
But then we come to a crossroads, unsure,
Of which way to turn and what's in store.

Do we follow our hearts or listen to our head,
Do we take the safe route or one less traveled instead?
For every decision we make on this journey of life,
Can lead us to happiness or lead to strife.

So we stand at the crossroads, searching for a sign,
Wondering which path will be truly divine,
And though the choice may not always be clear,
We must trust ourselves and let go of our fear.

For life is a journey, full of twists and turns,
And it's up to us to take the reins and learn,
To make the most of every opportunity,
And create a life that's filled with unity.

So go with the flow or seek directions anew,
For only you can decide what's best for you,
But at every crossroads, remember this,
Your choices will shape your journey and your bliss.

THE PATH AHEAD

As I walk along this winding road,
The future still remains untold,
Should I trust my intuition's hold,
Or let the world's opinions take their toll?

The path ahead seems so unclear,
Uncertainty and doubt fill me with fear,
Should I let go and just go with the flow,
Or chart my course and let my soul glow?

My heart aches with indecision,
As I weigh the choices with precision,
But deep within, I hear a voice,
Guiding me to make the right choice.

So I take a step, and then another,
Trusting my instincts, and not another,
For though the journey may be rough,
I'll find my way, and that's enough.

So let us embrace the unknown,
And let our spirits be shown,
For in the end, the journey's goal,
Is to find ourselves and make us whole.

THE SEARCH WITHIN:

Lost in the chaos, I wandered aimlessly
Uncertain of my path, my destiny
In search of meaning, I sought out my soul
Hoping to find my purpose, my goal

Days turned to weeks; weeks turned to years
As I searched for my passion, my fears.
Doubt crept in, a shadow on my mind,
As I wondered if my purpose I'd ever find

But deep within, a spark did glow
A flame that burned, with a steady flow
It whispered to me, calling out my name
Guiding me on, never leading me astray

And so I followed, with faith in my heart
Trusting the journey, right from the start
With each step, my purpose became clear.
A purpose that filled me, with joy and cheer

For I found my calling, my reason to be,
To inspire, to create, to set my soul free.
And now I know, my purpose is my guide,
Leading me forward, on this journey of life.

CHASING DREAMS, FIGHTING REALITY"

When I dream of soaring high,
And reaching for the endless sky,
The world below calls out to me,
Demanding I stay grounded, endlessly.

With obligations pulling me back,
I'm caught in a constant tug of war,
Between the things I need to do,
And the things I long for more.

I strive to find my true purpose,
To follow my heart and blaze my trail,
But the weight of responsibility,
Can sometimes feel like an unbreakable jail.

Yet still, I hold onto hope,
And keep my dreams within my sight,
For I know that with each step I take,
I am one step closer to the light.

And though the journey may be long,
And the path may not always be clear,
I'll keep on walking towards my purpose,
With determination and without fear.

For when I finally reach the end,
And look back on the road I've tread,
I'll know that every step I took,
Was a step towards the life I led.

WHISPERS OF THE HEART,

Whispers of the heart, so soft and true,
Echo through the chambers, a song for you,
A melody of hope, a message of love,
Guiding your steps, to the heavens above.

Whispers of the heart, a gentle breeze,
Stirring your soul, with a sense of ease,
A soothing touch, a calming embrace,
Filling your being, with divine grace.

Whispers of the heart, a sacred voice,
Speaking of wisdom, an enlightened choice,
Guiding you forward, on the path of light,
Illuminating your way, through the darkest of night.

Listen closely, to the whispers of the heart,
For they will guide you, to where you must start,
With courage and faith, take the first step,
And let the whispers of the heart, help you to find your true depth.

GRATEFUL

Grateful for the sun that shines,
And the stars that light the night.
Grateful for the moon that glows,
And the birds that take to flight.

Grateful for the air we breathe,
And the water that we drink.
Grateful for the food we eat,
And the love that makes us think.

Grateful for the friends we have,
And the family by our side.
Grateful for the memories made,
And the moments we'll abide.

Grateful for the lessons learned,
And the paths we've traveled down.
Grateful for the challenges faced,
And the strength we have found.

Grateful for this life we live,
And the beauty that surrounds.
Grateful for each day we have,
And the blessings that abound.

AWAKENING OF SPRING

Spring is near, the air is sweet,
The daffodils are at our feet.
Their golden petals shine so bright,
A joyful sight, a pure delight.

They rise up from the winter's sleep,
Their beauty makes the heart leap.
They dance and sway in the gentle breeze,
A symbol of hope and new beginnings, please.

Their fragrance fills the fresh spring air,
A sweet aroma beyond compare.
With each bloom, a new life starts,
And hope fills every heart.

So let us take a moment to admire,
These precious flowers, so bold and tireless.
They bring us joy and hope anew,
And remind us of the beauty that surrounds us too.

DAFFODILS

Daffodils blooming bright and bold,
A symbol of life and hope untold.
Yet sudden snow, a cruel surprise,
Their fate uncertain, their beauty disguised.

Struggling to rise, to find their way,
Through the frozen blanket, they still sway.
Their will to survive, a wonder to see,
Like humans in crises, they fight to be free.

Their resilience a lesson to learn,
In the face of adversity, to still yearn.
For the sun to shine, for warmth to be found,
To break free from the cold and stand on ground.

Daffodils in snow, a sight to behold,
Their spirit unbroken, their story told.
Of strength, of courage, of hope and grace,
In times of turmoil, to still find a place.

SURVIVING THE UNEXPECTED

In the midst of chaos and strife,
When the world around us is rife
With uncertainty, fear, and doubt,
We find ourselves struggling about.

But there's a strength within us all,
A resilience that helps us stand tall,
And face the challenges that we meet,
Even when they knock us off our feet.

For we are survivors, through and through,
With the power to endure and renew,
To rise up from the ashes of defeat,
And find a way to make life sweet.

It's not easy, this journey we're on,
With so many obstacles to overcome,
But we keep moving forward, step by step,
With the courage to face whatever's left.

So when the unexpected comes our way,
And we feel like we've lost our say,
We remember the strength within our soul,
And keep on going, towards our goal.

For we are survivors, through and through,
And nothing can ever break us in two,
As long as we hold on to hope and love,
And keep our eyes fixed on the One above.

LOST IN THE MAZE

Confusion reigns inside my mind,
A tangled mess I cannot unwind,
The more I try, the worse it gets,
A never-ending cycle of regrets.

I search for answers, but they're elusive,
A puzzle that's too complex to be conclusive,
My thoughts scatter like leaves in the wind,
Lost and scattered, with no way to rescind.

Each decision feels like a gamble,
A risk that's taken with a shaky handle,
And in the end, the result is the same,
A feeling of loss, of defeat, of shame.

Yet still, I press on through the haze,
Hoping to emerge from this chaotic maze,
For I know that clarity will come,
And with it, the chance to feel whole and one.

So I'll take each step with careful thought,
And try to navigate the confusion I've wrought,
For in the end, I know I'll find my way,
And clarity will come to me one day.

LOST IN THE FOG OF CONFUSION

Lost in the fog of confusion,
A labyrinth of thoughts and illusions.
The mind races with no clear conclusion,
A constant battle, an endless intrusion.

Questions abound, with no answers in sight,
Uncertainty grips with all its might.
Doubt and fear cloud every decision,
Leaving no room for clear vision.

In this maze, the heart can lead astray,
Emotions deceive and create dismay.
Yet reason beckons to find the way,
To break through the fog and find the ray.

So hold on tight, and trust the inner voice,
The one that guides with a steady poise.
With patience and perseverance, the fog will clear,
And the path forward will slowly appear.

For in the end, confusion can be a friend,
A chance to pause, reflect, and amend.
To find new paths, and grow in strength,
To navigate the unknown, and go to any length.

So let confusion be the catalyst,
To propel forward, and never resist.
To embrace the journey, with all its confusion,
And emerge stronger, with newfound resolution.

THE WEIGHT OF GUILT

Guilt, a heavy burden to bear,
A weight on my chest, a constant affair.
The past lingers, haunting my mind,
The mistakes I made, so hard to unwind.

Remorse fills me, an ache in my heart,
For the pain I caused, for the hurt I impart.
I wish I could turn back time, make things right,
But the consequences remain, a never-ending fight.

The weight of guilt, a crushing force,
Pulling me down, with no remorse.
I try to shake it off, to let it go,
But it clings to me, a never-ending woe.

I must face it, own up to my mistakes,
Accept the consequences, no matter the stakes.
I must learn from it, grow from the pain,
And make amends, to ease the strain.

Guilt may never truly go away,
But it can be managed, day by day.
I'll carry it with me, as a reminder to be,
A better person, for all to see.

LEAVING THEM BEHIND

Leaving them behind, it breaks my heart,
As I head out to work, right from the start.
I know they need me, my babies so dear,
But I need to earn, to allay my fear.

Guilt weighs me down, like a heavy stone,
As I leave my children, to work alone.
Their faces etched, in my mind I see,
With pleading eyes, they look up to me.

But I have to go, it's a fact of life,
To provide for them, and ease their strife.
I pray they understand, why I must leave,
And hope they don't, feel too much grief.

Their smiles, their hugs, their little voices,
I carry them with me, making my choices.
I work harder, for their sake and mine,
Hoping to give them a future, so divine.

But as the day ends, and I head back home,
I long to see them, no longer to roam.
I rush to their arms, to hold them tight,
To make up for the absence, with all my might.

The guilt remains, a constant companion,
But I remind myself, it's not abandonment.
I'm doing what I must, for my family's good,
And hope they understand, as I knew they would.

Leaving them behind, it breaks my heart,
But I know deep down, it's the best part.
For when I see them, with a smile so wide,
I know the sacrifice, is worth the pride.

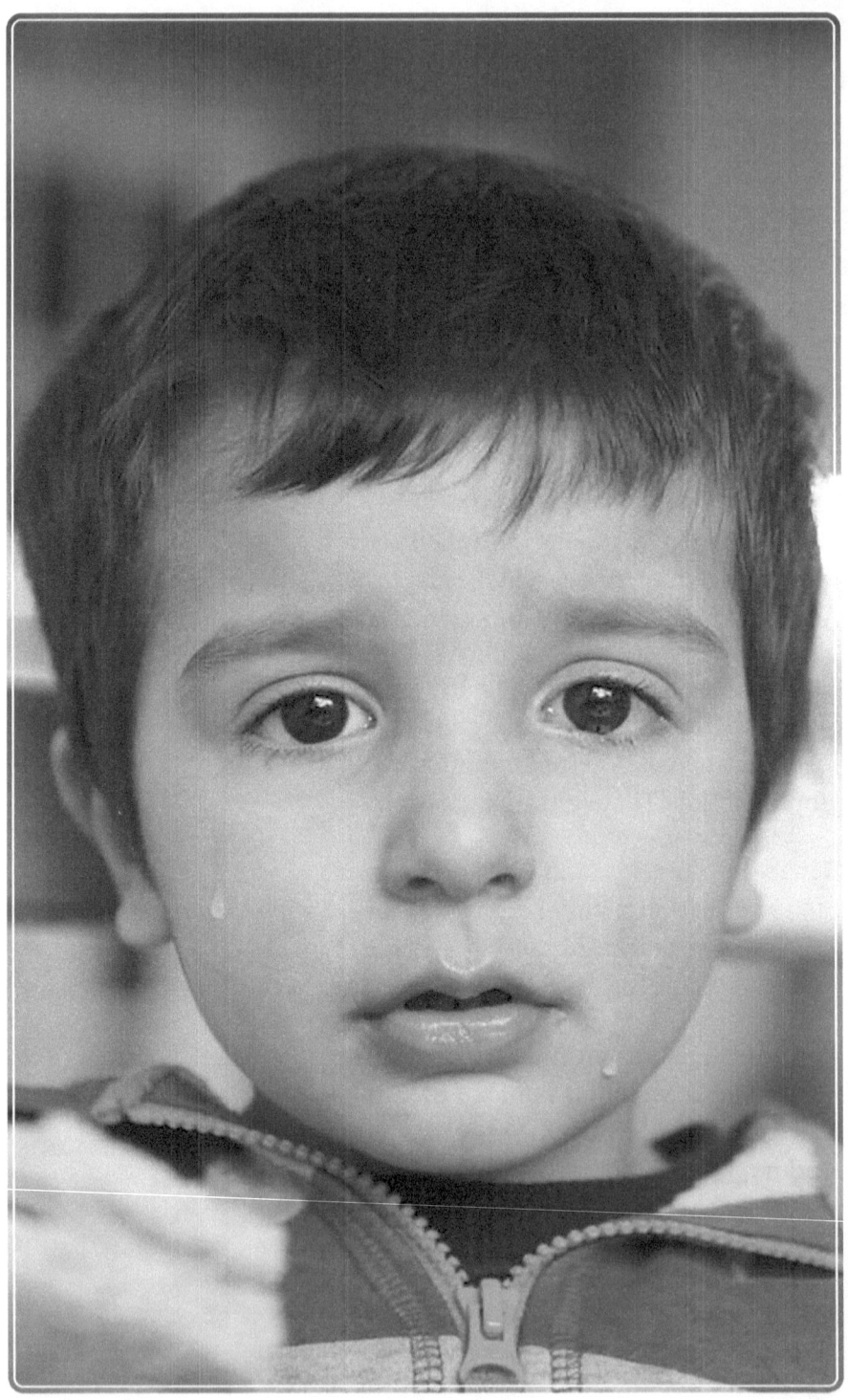

THE HAUNTING GUILT OF A MOTHER

As she left her little one in the nursery that day,
Her heart felt heavy, her mind in disarray.
Though she had to go out and work to make ends meet,
The thought of leaving her baby was hard to defeat.

As she walked away, she turned around to see,
Her child howling, crying, longing to be free.
The attendant tried to calm him, but he just wouldn't rest,
And in that moment, her guilt consumed her chest.

She wondered if she had made the right decision,
To leave her child in the care of a stranger, with no vision.
She questioned herself, and her role as a mother,
Was it worth it, to earn for the family, and not be with the other?

The overwhelming emotions haunted her all day,
As she worked hard to make a living, to earn her pay.
But her mind was with her child, who she left behind,
Was he treated well, or rudely, did he get what he pined?

She couldn't wait to rush back to the nursery that eve,
To see her baby, to hold him close, and to relieve,
The guilt that had consumed her, all through the day,
And to promise herself, that she'd never leave him astray.

The haunting guilt of a mother, who has to leave,
Is a burden that's hard to bear, and hard to relieve.
But the love for her child, and the hope for a better tomorrow,
Keeps her going, and helps her through the sorrow.

TOY FOR THE PAIN

A mother's heart aches with every goodbye,
As she leaves her child to the nursery's cry.
Her little one howls as she walks away,
And the guilt weighs heavy, day after day.

But she buys him toys to ease the pain,
Hoping it will make up for her absence again.
She wishes she could stay by his side,
And be the one to wipe away every tear he's cried.

The toys become a symbol of her love,
A tangible reminder from above.
That she's doing all she can for her little boy,
And her heart breaks with every separation ploy.

But the guilt still haunts her every night,
As she pictures her son's helpless plight.
She wonders if he's being treated well,
Or if the nursery attendant's actions are hell.

The emotions overwhelm her, time and again,
And she struggles to find a way to ease the pain.
But she knows that her love will always remain,
A constant presence, even in moments of strain.

So she kisses her son goodbye with a heavy heart,
And hopes that the toys will play a small part.
In making him feel loved and cared for each day,
Until she's with him again, in every possible way.

SHARED RESPONSIBILITY

As a mother, I carry the weight
Of raising our kids, day by day
But I long for a partner by my side
To share the load and help provide

I ask my husband to lend a hand
To take the kids and help them stand
But he sees it as a job for me
And says, „I have work, you see"

So I soldier on, with tears in my eyes
Feeling the weight of every sigh
I know that it's not fair or just
To shoulder this burden, all on my own

But I can't let my kids down
And so I wear the invisible crown
Of a mother, who works day and night
To ensure that her kids stay bright

I long for a day when he'll see
That raising kids is a joint responsibility
And until then, I'll keep on trying
To balance it all, without denying

The love and care that my kids need
To grow up happy, healthy and free
For though it's hard, I'll never stop
Giving them all that I've got.

THE EMPTY CHAIR

He stumbles in the door, reeking of booze,
A man who prefers the bottle to family news.
His wife and kids sit, waiting in despair,
Hoping for a sign that he might care.

But night after night, he's lost in his drink,
As if he's in a trance, he can barely think.
His family's needs, they fall by the wayside,
While he drowns his sorrows in a bottle he hides.

The kids go to bed without a goodnight kiss,
While his wife sits alone, reminiscing on bliss.
She wonders where her husband has gone,
And why he's content with drinking until dawn.

But she knows deep down, it's more than just the booze,
It's a lack of responsibility and being true.
She longs for a man who can stand up and be strong,
And be a partner in life, not just a drunk all day long.

TWISTED LOVE

He twists my words and makes me doubt
My memories and what I'm all about
He says it's my fault, I'm just confused
But his lies and manipulation leave me feeling used

He tells me I'm crazy, I'm losing my mind
That I'm the problem, that I'm hard to find
He makes me feel small, like I'm in the wrong
But his behavior is what's been going on all along

He denies what he's done, and tells me I'm wrong
He tries to convince me I'm not really strong
But I see through his lies, I know what's real
And I won't let his manipulation steal

My sense of self, my confidence and pride
I'll break free from his gaslighting and lies inside
I'll stand tall and speak my truth with conviction
And find my way back to my own intuition.

LEFT BEHIND BY LOVE'S PROMISE

Alone in the room, I feel the emptiness inside,
The one I love, the one I need, is nowhere by my side.
He promised to be there for me, through sickness and in health,
But when I needed him the most, he was out with someone else.

I feel the ache inside my heart, the pain it brings me still,
To know that I am all alone, when I need him to fulfill.
The promises he made to me, seem to fade away,
And I'm left with nothing but the hurt, that's here to stay.

He tells me that he loves me, and that he'll never stray,
But when the time comes to prove it, he always looks away.
I feel so cheated and alone, in this life we share,
And I wonder if he'll ever see, how much I really care.

I wish that he could understand, the way his actions hurt,
To know that I'm in pain, and it's only getting worse.
But he's so caught up in his own world, he doesn't see the signs,
And I'm left here to pick up the pieces, of a love that's left behind.

So I'll keep on holding on, to the love that we once knew,
And pray that someday he'll realize, how much I need him too.
For the pain of being alone, is a burden I can't bear,
And I hope that he'll come back to me, and show me that he cares.

TWISTED GAMES OF DECEIT

He speaks with words of honeyed lies,
And paints a picture in her eyes,
Of love and trust and loyalty,
A perfect match, for all to see.

But in her heart, she's made to believe,
That he's the one who'll never leave,
And so she stays, and takes the pain,
And hopes that love will still remain.

But every time he speaks his lies,
She feels the tears fill up her eyes,
And wonders how she got so blind,
To the manipulations of his kind.

She's scared to leave and scared to stay,
For fear of what he'll do or say,
And so she's trapped within his hold,
A prisoner of a story untold.

But deep inside, she knows the truth,
That love and trust should never soothe,
The wounds that he's inflicted so,
And she's determined now to go.

To break the chains and find her way,
To freedom from his sick display,
And in her heart, she'll hold the key,
To a life where she'll finally be free.

A WOMAN'S SECRET LONGING

She wakes up every morning to the same routine,
A life of servitude, with little room to dream,
She tends to her family, day in and day out,
And though she loves them, she's left with doubt.

For deep inside, a fire burns bright,
A yearning for more, a desire to take flight,
To live a life with purpose and zeal,
And not just play a role, that's lost its appeal.

And though she plays her role as wife and bore,
Her heart is empty, and love's not in store.
For duty binds her to this life she leads,
But true passion and joy are what she needs.

She longs for more than just a daily grind,
To break free from the chains that bind,
And find a life that's truly hers,
With happiness and love that endures.

For she's more than just a mother and a wife,
And wants to live a meaningful life,
With purpose and passion, and dreams come true,
And not just living to please her family too.

So she'll take the steps to find her way,
And break free from the life that's gray,
And though it's hard, she'll make the leap,
And find the joy and love she seeks.

THE STRENGTH TO SOAR BEYOND DUTY'S CALL

The weight of her burdens heavy to bear,
As she's used by her family without a care,
Her body aches from the years of toil,
And she's left with little time to recoil.

She's given birth to many a child,
Her body worn and tired, yet still she smiled,
For it was her duty, her place in life,
To be a mother and a dutiful wife.

But now as the years have passed her by,
She longs for freedom, to spread her wings and fly,
To be more than just a caretaker and a nurse,
To find a life that's fulfilling and diverse.

Her husband, he tries to understand,
But the years of service have taken their toll on this land,
And though she loves him, she wants something more,
To be more than just a wife and a bore.

So she dreams of the life that could have been,
Of the chances lost and the roads not taken,
And though she bears no ill will towards her kin,
She knows her future is hers to awaken.

For she's more than just a wife and a mother,
She's a person with dreams and aspirations to discover,
And though the journey ahead may be hard,
She knows she's strong, and can go far.

FINDING GRACE

She mourns the loss of a life once held,
A child unborn, forever stilled,
And though her heart is filled with pain,
She's met with coldness and disdain.

For in the eyes of those around,
She's seen as cursed, possessed, unsound,
And so she's shunned and left alone,
Her sorrow left to fester and groan.

She's told to lock herself away,
To keep her shadow, and her face at bay,
For fear that spirits may take hold,
And curse the family with a fate foretold.

Her cries are met with harsh rebuke,
As if her pain is just a ploy to duke,
And though they mourn the baby gone,
Her suffering is ignored and shunned.

But she knows deep down inside,
That her pain and grief can't be denied,
And though the world may turn its back,
She'll find the strength to get back on track.

For in her heart, she knows the truth,
That she's not cursed, but just in need of proof,
That love and compassion still exist,
And in her sorrow, she'll persist.

So she'll rise above the hurt and pain,
And find a way to heal again,
And though her loss can never be replaced,
She'll find a way to live with grace.

SUFFOCATING SILENCE:
THE STRUGGLE OF A MOTHER'S LOST CHOICES"

She thought it was for the best,
To abort the child and give him rest,
But with each passing day, she feels the weight,
Of the decision made, and the child's fate.

Her partner asked, and she agreed,
To abort the child, for financial need,
But now she's lost count, with a heart full of sorrow,
Wondering if it was right, for a better tomorrow.

With each passing day, the guilt consumes,
The loss of the child, it still looms,
And though she has two sons, she feels incomplete,
As the weight of her decisions, she can't defeat.

Her partner's words, they haunt her soul,
As the pain of her losses take their toll,
And though she tries to move on and forget,
The weight of her choices, she can't neglect.

For the loss of her children, it's a burden to bear,
And the guilt and the pain, they're always there,
But she'll keep moving forward, with her head held high,
And hope that someday, the weight will subside.

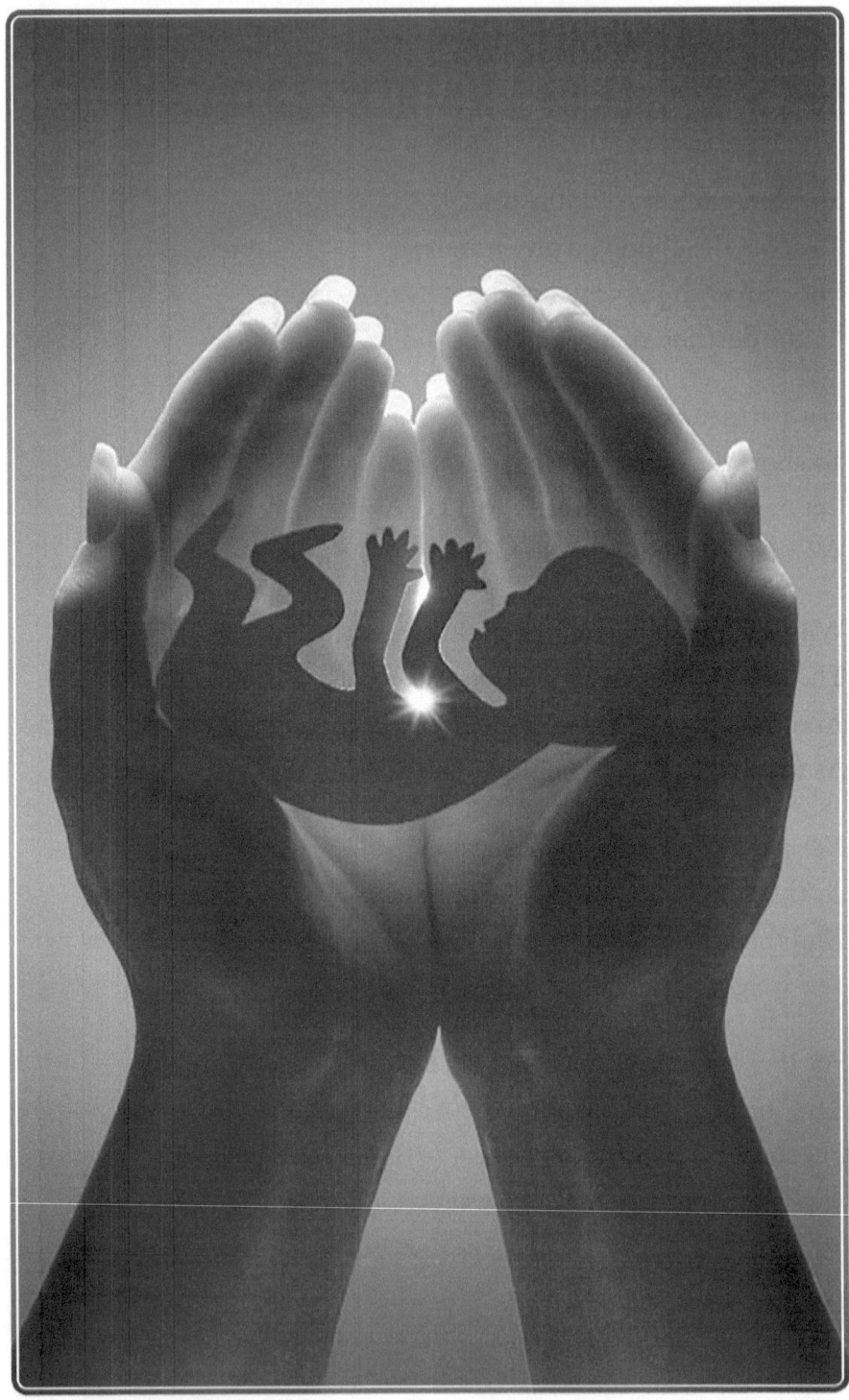

SILENCED SORROW: A WOMAN'S PAIN UNHEARD

She's asked to choose, to make a call,
To end a life before it can crawl,
And though her heart is filled with doubt,
She's pressured to make the choice and bow out.

Her partner's reasons, they seem sound,
But the weight of loss is what she's found,
For with each abortion, a piece of her dies,
And the guilt and sadness, it multiplies.

She looks at her sons, and wonders why,
She agreed to end the lives of those who'd never cry,
And though she knows it's not all on her,
The pain and guilt, it's hard to endure.

Her heart is heavy, her soul is tired,
And the grief, it can't be easily acquired,
For in her mind, she's lost a piece,
Of what it means to feel at peace.

But she knows that she must find a way,
To heal the hurt and brighten the gray,
And though the guilt may never fully fade,
She'll find a way to live unafraid.

For in her heart, she knows the truth,
That she's more than just a decision, uncouth,
And though her partner may not understand,
She'll find a way to take back her own command.

So she'll rise above the pain and strife,
And find a way to reclaim her life,
And though the scars may never fully heal,
She'll find a way to trust what she feels.

CONFRONTING FEAR

Fear, the emotion that grips our soul,
Its icy grip can take a toll,
It can stop us from doing what we must,
Leaving us in the dust.

But what if we confront our fear?
And face it with a brave, determined cheer?
What if we look it in the eye,
And refuse to let it make us shy?

For when we confront our fear,
And refuse to let it make us disappear,
We find that it loses its power,
And we can face any challenge, any hour.

We find that we are stronger than we thought,
That we can conquer any fear, any fraught,
We find that we can rise above,
And live a life filled with love.

So let us confront our fear,
And face it with a brave, determined cheer,
For in doing so, we find our true strength,
And can go the distance, any length.

GUIDING THE FLAMES:
TURNING ANGER INTO ACTION

Anger, a fire that burns inside,
A feeling that we cannot hide,
It can consume us, tear us apart,
Leave us with a heavy heart.

But what if we take that fire,
And use it to build, to inspire?
What if we channel that energy,
And turn it into something mighty?

For when we harness our anger,
And use it constructively, with fervor,
We find that it can fuel our passion,
And help us make a positive action.

We find that we can stand up for what's right,
And make a difference, with all our might,
We find that our anger can be a force,
That helps us chart a better course.

So let us use our anger wisely,
And turn it into something lively,
For in doing so, we can make a change,
And our world can become a better range.

WHEN YOU FEEL POWERLESS:
HOW TO TRAIN YOUR BRAIN TO SEEK SOLUTIONS

It's easy to feel powerless when others control your life,
Their actions can cause anger, pain, and strife,
But even in the midst of such a difficult situation,
There are ways to train your brain to seek solutions.

Don't dwell on what you cannot control,
Instead, focus on your role,
Take small steps and build momentum gradually,
This will help you feel more in charge, more free.

Take a deep breath and focus on the present,
Use mindfulness to stay centered and present,
This can help you stay calm, clear-headed,
And make it easier to find a way forward.

Don't hesitate to seek support from those who care,
Their guidance and encouragement can help you dare,
They can offer you a fresh perspective,
And help you see the situation more objectively.

Be kind to yourself and practice self-compassion,
It's not your fault if others treat you with aggression,
Remember that you deserve to be treated with respect,
And that you have the power to make your life perfect.

When others control you, remember this,
You still have agency, you're not a powerless wisp,
You can train your brain to seek solutions, to find a way,
And create a life that's filled with joy, each and every day.

LOVE UNKNOWN

Love was a stranger, a mystery to me,
No one had shown it, no one had set it free,
All had hidden motives, a price to pay,
A game of give and take, a role to play.

But then came my sons, my little rays of light,
Their love was pure, a beacon shining bright,
No strings attached, no conditions to meet,
A selfless love, so pure and sweet.

Their smiles, their laughter, their gentle touch,
They taught me the meaning, I wanted so much,
Love is not a game, not a tool to wield,
It's a bond that's strong, a shield that's sealed.

Their love opened my heart, unlocked the door,
I felt it flow, deep to my core,
And in that moment, I understood,
The power of love, so strong and good.

No more hidden motives, no more games to play,
Love is not a price, it's not a debt to pay,
It's a gift that's given, a blessing to share,
A bond that's unbreakable, a love that's rare.

So now I know, love is not unknown,
It's something I cherish, something I've grown,
Thanks to my sons, who taught me to see,
The real meaning of love, and what it means to be free.

A MOTHER'S LOVE

A mother's heart is full of love,
A love that's pure, sent from above,
She dreams of finding love anew,
But stays loyal, for the sake of her two.

Her marriage, it's not what she hoped for,
She longs for more, for something more,
But in her heart, she knows the truth,
Her sons come first, their happiness the proof.

She can't bear the thought of causing them pain,
Of bringing another man into their domain,
She knows it's not about what she wants,
It's about protecting them, and their hearts.

So she stays true, she stays loyal,
For the sake of her boys, she stays royal,
Her love for them, it knows no bounds,
A love that's fierce, and forever profound.

She dreams of finding love, a love that's new,
But for now, she'll love her sons, and see them through,
She'll be their rock, their guide, and their friend,
A mother's love, that will never end.

A MOTHER'S STRENGTH

A mother's love knows no bounds,
It stretches far and wide, without a sound,
But now her sons have grown up tall,
And she expects her husband to stand up tall.

For years, she's been the rock of the family,
Nurturing and guiding, with love and empathy,
But now it's time for her to take a back seat,
And for her husband to show their sons the way to meet.

But as she looks to him, she feels betrayed,
As he refuses to play his part, to give aid,
And once again, she must be the pillar of strength,
For her sons, who now must go to great lengths.

They need to be strong, to build their own lives,
To overcome challenges, and rise above the strife,
And so she stands strong, once again,
A mother's love, that will never wane.

Though her heart may ache, and her soul may tire,
She never loses sight of her sons' desire,
To carve their own path, to make their own way,
To be successful, in their own way.

For them, she will always be there,
To lift them up, and help them prepare,
To face the world, with all its trials,
And build a future, that's worth their while.

And though she wishes support was more by her side,
She knows her love and strength will never subside,
For her children, who mean the world to her,
A mother's unwavering love, that will always endure.

GROWING IN GRATITUDE: A MINDSET SHIFT

Every day is a blessing, that's what they say,
But it's easy to forget, in the hustle and fray,
We get caught up in our worries and stress,
And forget to appreciate, all that we possess.

But when we start to cultivate, a mindset of gratitude,
We start to see the world, in a different attitude,
We begin to notice, all the good that surrounds,
And see the beauty, that abounds.

We start to feel more content, with what we have,
And appreciate, the moments that make us glad,
We begin to focus, on the positive and bright,
And let go of worries, that consume us at night.

We become mindful, of our thoughts and emotions,
And realize the power, of positive notions,
We see the world, through a different lens,
And cherish the moments, with family and friends.

Growing in gratitude, takes time and practice,
But the rewards are worth it, as we shift our axis,
We become more joyful, and more at peace,
And find happiness, that's lasting and deep.

So let's take a moment, to count our blessings each day,
And appreciate, all the good that comes our way,
For in doing so, we will grow and thrive,
In a world that's full of beauty, and that's truly alive.

THE POWER OF FRIENDS WHO STAND BY YOU

In the depths of despair, when all hope seemed lost,
And the world seemed cruel, like a tempest it tossed,
There were friends by my side, who silently stayed,
Their presence and care, an unspoken parade.

They didn't say much, but their presence was felt,
Their support and love, like a balm that can melt,
Away the pain and the worry, that consumed me whole,
Their silent strength, helping me regain control.

They listened without judgment, and held my hand,
In their gentle embrace, I found a safe land,
Where I could be myself, and let down my guard,
Their unwavering support, a comforting card.

They reminded me, that I was not alone,
And that I could count on them, to help me atone,
For my mistakes and my flaws, that made me human,
They showed me love, that was genuine and proven.

With their help and their care, I found my way,
And emerged from the darkness, into the light of day,
Their friendship, a gift that I cherish each moment,
For they silently stood by me, with unwavering commitment.

SUNBEAMS OF HAPPINESS

When the world seems bleak, and all hope is lost,
When the weight of the world seems like too high a cost,
Remember to think of happy thoughts, and let them shine,
Through your face like sunbeams, and all will be just fine.

Think of the laughter of children, and the joy that they bring,
Think of the melody of music, and the way it can make your heart sing,
Think of the beauty of nature, and the colors of the sky,
Think of the love of family, and the warmth of a close tie.

Let these thoughts fill your mind, and your heart with light,
Let them shine through your face, and dispel the darkness of night,
For even in the midst of chaos, and the storms that may come,
There's always a glimmer of hope, a light that can't be undone.

So hold onto those happy thoughts, and let them guide your way,
And let them shine through your face, like the sun on a summer's day,
For when you radiate positivity, and let your spirit soar,
The world will be a brighter place, and you'll find so much more. a title

BLOOM AND SHINE

Bloom where life plants you, let your light shine,
For even in darkness, your beauty will align,
With the rays of hope, that shine from within,
And make a difference, with every grin.

Spread your petals, and embrace the sun,
Let it nourish your soul, and help you become,
A symbol of grace, in this chaotic world,
A beacon of love, that leaves hearts unfurled.

For when you bloom, you bring joy to those around,
And make their sorrows, and worries, unbound,
You give them hope, and a reason to smile,
And inspire them to bloom, in their own unique style.

So don't be afraid, to grow in your own way,
To spread your love, and kindness, every day,
For wherever you go, you can make a difference,
And be the reason, for someone's brightest radiance.

Bloom where life plants you, and let your light shine,
Be the flower of hope, in a world that needs a sign,
Of love, of joy, of peace, and of grace,
And inspire others, to bloom in their own space.

BELIEVE IN YOURSELF

If you're searching for meaning, for something to believe,
Start with yourself, for that's where it all leads.
For within you lies a universe of potential,
A spark of light, a flame that's essential.

Believe in your dreams, in the power of your will,
In the strength of your spirit, that nothing can kill.
Believe in your heart, in the beat of its rhythm,
In the love that it holds, that's never a victim.

Don't look to others, for validation or proof,
For the truth that you seek, lies within you, aloof.
Be your own guiding light, your own source of hope,
And watch as your world, begins to transform and elope.

For when you believe in yourself, anything's possible,
The doors start to open, and the barriers become solvable.
You become the reason, for your own success,
The catalyst for change, that's bold and fearless.

So if you want something to believe in, start with yourself,
And let the magic unfold, like a book on a shelf.
Bloom where life plants you, and spread joy with a smile,
For in believing in yourself, you'll go the extra mile.

"FINDING STRENGTH WITHIN"

Believe in yourself, and all that you can be,
For the power lies within, deep inside you and me.
It's not in the stars, or in some grand design,
But in your own heart, and in your own mind.

Don't look to others, for validation or proof,
For their beliefs and dreams, may not match your own truth.
Follow your passions, and listen to your soul,
And let your spirit guide you, towards your ultimate goal.

You are capable of greatness, beyond what you know,
Just trust in yourself, and let your confidence grow.
Take risks and chances, and learn from your mistakes,
For they are just steppingstones, towards the path you will take.

So if you want something to believe in, start with yourself,
And watch as your life unfolds, like a book on a shelf.
With each page that turns, and each new chapter begun,
You'll see that the power of belief, can help you overcome.

FADING STRENGTH, RENEWED RESOLVE

In the realm of exhaustion, weariness prevails,
As time marches on, energy gradually fails.
The demands of the world, relentless and vast,
Leave one feeling drained, as the days go past.

The weight of responsibilities takes its toll,
Fatigue seeps in, consuming the soul.
With each passing moment, weariness grows,
A longing for respite, a moment of repose.

The body aches, the mind seeks rest,
Yearning for solace, to feel truly blessed.
But amidst the weariness, a spark remains,
A glimmer of hope broke through the strains.

For within the tiredness, strength can be found,
In moments of stillness, new energy is crowned.
With self-care and balance, rejuvenation thrives,
And weariness retreats, as vitality arrives.

So let the weariness be a temporary state,
A reminder to pause and recalibrate.
For in replenishing the spirit and finding reprieve,
We overcome exhaustion and truly achieve

"Echoes of the Soul" is a moving collection of poems that explores the many facets of life's journey. Through vivid imagery and heartfelt language, the poems in this collection reflect on themes such as love, loss, self-discovery, and resilience. From the soaring highs to the crushing lows, these poems speak to the human experience in all its complexity and beauty. Whether you are seeking comfort in times of struggle or simply looking for inspiration, this collection is sure to resonate with you on a deep, emotional level.

Look forward to the next batch of villanelle poems, which is an ancient form of poetry.

N A M R I T A , the talented author of the captivating poetry collection *"Echoes of the Soul,"* is a seasoned educator and a dedicated mindfulness and well-being coach with over two decades of experience. Throughout her illustrious career, she has nurtured young minds, instilled a love for learning, and encouraged personal growth in her students.

As an artist specializing in oil, acrylic, and charcoal paintings, Namrita possesses a unique ability to translate her artistic expression onto the canvas. Her paintings serve as a source of inspiration for her writing, infusing her poems with vivid imagery and a deep sense of visual storytelling Namrita's journey as a writer began with the creation of short stories and engaging blogs, which provided a platform for her to explore her creativity and share her thoughts on various subjects. Over time, her writing evolved to include poetry, a powerful medium through which she could delve into the depths of human emotions and capture the intricacies of the human experience.

With *"Echoes of the Soul,"* Namrita offers her readers a glimpse into her inner world, where words dance with grace and emotions are laid bare. Her poems are a reflection of her profound understanding of the human condition, intertwining themes of love, resilience, self-discovery, and the pursuit of inner peace.

Namrita's expertise as an educator and mindfulness coach shines through in her poetry, as she encourages readers to embrace mindfulness, find solace in the present moment, and embark on a journey of self-reflection and personal growth. Her words have the power to heal, inspire, and ignite a spark of profound transformation within those who immerse themselves in the pages of her book.

As you embark on the poetic voyage within *"Echoes of the Soul,"* allow Namrita's artistry and wisdom to guide you on a profound exploration of the human spirit. Her words will awaken your senses, stir your emotions, and leave an indelible imprint on your soul, reminding you of the limitless power of artistic expression and the boundless beauty that resides within.